LIVING WITH DISORDERS AND DISABILITIES

LIVING WITH OCD

by Michelle Garcia Andersen

San Diego, CA

© 2019 ReferencePoint Press, Inc.
Printed in the United States

For more information, contact:
ReferencePoint Press, Inc.
PO Box 27779
San Diego, CA 92198
www.ReferencePointPress.com

ALL RIGHTS RESERVED.

No part of this work covered by the copyright hereon may be reproduced or used in any form or by any means—graphic, electronic, or mechanical, including photocopying, recording, taping, web distribution, or information storage retrieval systems—without the written permission of the publisher.

LIBRARY OF CONGRESS CATALOGING-IN-PUBLICATION DATA

Name: Andersen, Michelle Garcia, author.
Title: Living with OCD / By Michelle Garcia Andersen.
Description: San Diego, CA : ReferencePoint Press, Inc., [2019] | Series:
 Living with Disorders and Disabilities | Audience: Grade 9 to 12. |
 Includes bibliographical references and index.
Identifiers: LCCN 2018011538 (print) | LCCN 2018011760 (ebook) | ISBN
 9781682824849 (ebook) | ISBN 9781682824832 (hardback)
Subjects: LCSH: Obsessive-compulsive disorder—Juvenile literature.
Classification: LCC RC533 (ebook) | LCC RC533 .A53 2019 (print) | DDC
 616.85/227—dc23
LC record available at https://lccn.loc.gov/2018011538

CONTENTS

Introduction
Two Stories of OCD — 4

Chapter One
What Is OCD? — 10

Chapter Two
OCD Symptoms and Diagnosis — 24

Chapter Three
The Impact of OCD — 40

Chapter Four
Treatment for OCD — 56

Source Notes — 70
For Further Research — 74
Index — 76
Image Credits — 79
About the Author — 80

INTRODUCTION

TWO STORIES OF OCD

Trey woke to the smell of bacon. He wanted to jump out of bed and run downstairs like he used to do. Instead, he reached for some tissues and placed them over his dresser drawer knobs as he opened the top drawer. He grabbed a pair of socks and put them on, careful not to touch his bare feet with his hands. As he headed for the door, he looked at the bottoms of his feet. His socks looked clean, but they felt dirty. Back to the dresser he went.

Trey grabbed more tissues, took a new pair of socks from the dresser, and put them on in place of the other pair. His mom was calling. He was going to be late for school again. Trey made his way back to the door but couldn't resist the urge to check the bottoms of his feet. He was certain his socks were covered in germs. Trey started to sweat. He hurried back to the dresser and changed into yet another pair.

Excessive fear of dirt and contamination is a common obsession among people with OCD. Knowing the fear is irrational does not stop it.

Trey made it to the top of the stairs before he checked again. He knew this was irrational, but his brain kept telling him to check. He could *feel* the dirt seeping into his socks.

By the time he made his way downstairs, he wanted to inspect his feet again but couldn't risk having his mom see him do so. Breakfast was nearly over. Dirty dishes were scattered across the table. He knew the germs from the used forks and plates had made their way onto his plate. There was no way he could eat now. He ignored the rumbling in his stomach and slowly, deliberately, made his way toward

Some people with OCD are obsessed with having things be symmetrical. If something isn't in exact alignment, it can make them uncomfortable.

the back door to get his coat and shoes, constantly checking the bottoms of his feet as he went.

Emma's Story

Emma was a straight-A student. She sang in the school choir and had an after-school job at a grocery store. Emma was a perfectionist. Her locker was always immaculate. All her books were lined up by height.

One afternoon, she was counting stock in the canned food section of the grocery store. She noticed a can of beans facing backward. She adjusted it so the label faced forward and then proceeded with her inventory. She had a hard time regaining focus and kept losing count. Something was gnawing at her to go back and check the cans again. She glanced at the beans, looking for labels that weren't facing forward. She spotted one that was slightly off, so she adjusted the can. Then she started counting again. But that worried feeling returned. What if other cans were also facing the wrong direction? Emma stopped counting and began rearranging every can in the aisle. Once each one was facing forward and was lined up with the others, she continued with the inventory.

A customer came by and quickly grabbed some beans from the shelf. Emma stopped counting. She had to go back and realign the cans. Another customer bumped into the shelf with his cart, moving a few cans out of their rows, so Emma repeated her process. She knew she was wasting time and wished she could stop rearranging. Her pulse raced when she thought about what her boss would say when the inventory still wasn't done. But Emma felt trapped in the canned food aisle, unable to move forward, constantly readjusting the cans.

Defining OCD

Although Trey and Emma display different symptoms, they both suffer from the same condition: obsessive-compulsive disorder, more commonly referred to as OCD. The National Institute of Mental Health (NIMH) defines OCD as "a common, chronic and long-lasting disorder in which a person has uncontrollable, reoccurring thoughts (obsessions) and behaviors (compulsions) that he or she feels the urge to repeat over and over."[1]

> "OCD is a common, chronic and long-lasting disorder in which a person has uncontrollable, reoccurring thoughts (obsessions) and behaviors (compulsions) that he or she feels the urge to repeat over and over."[1]
>
> —National Institute of Mental Health

An abnormal fear of contamination makes normal daily activities difficult. Even eating meals at home can produce anxiety.

Trey had obsessive thoughts about contamination. His fear of germs and dirt kept him from doing what he wanted to do—going downstairs and eating breakfast. Emma was obsessed with everything being symmetrical, another common symptom of OCD. Her fixation with having every can aligned and facing forward prevented her from getting her work done.

People with OCD are aware that their obsessions are irrational and illogical. Says psychologist Lee Fitzgibbons, "People with OCD, children and adults alike, will often hide their symptoms for as long as possible, sometimes for years, even from their families."[2] There's a common feeling of embarrassment and shame associated with OCD.

8

When people with OCD experience obsessive thoughts, they can't simply turn them off. These thoughts can cause great anxiety. One man recounts what it felt like growing up with OCD: "The anxiety meant that even tying my shoes was hard. Taking a shower was an undertaking of epic proportions, and just eating dinner was a battle. I [became] the prisoner of an illness that held my mind in an iron grip."[3]

Trey's logical self knew he would be all right if his socks picked up a little dirt, but the rest of his brain said otherwise. He felt no choice but to recheck and replace his socks with new ones. Similarly, Emma knew no harm would come if cans of beans weren't in a straight line. But both Trey and Emma felt the need to relieve their stress by checking on what was bothering them. This is the compulsive part of the disorder.

Compulsions are the acts or rituals that a person does to make the obsessions go away. "Rituals feel like necessary tools for survival," says psychologist Tamar Chansky.[4] The problem with performing a ritual is that it provides only temporary relief. As soon as the ritual is completed, doubt creeps back in, and the brain repeats the cycle.

Psychiatry professor John March says, "When you understand that OCD is a true brain illness, you realize that having it is not a matter of choice and resolving it is not a matter of willpower."[5] Fortunately for those caught in the grip of OCD, treatments are available to lessen the severity of symptoms. Understanding OCD is the first step in learning how to manage it.

> "When you understand that OCD is a true brain illness, you realize that having it is not a matter of choice and resolving it is not a matter of willpower."[5]
>
> —John March, psychiatry professor

Chapter 1

WHAT IS OCD?

The term *OCD* has become common in today's popular culture. You've likely heard someone say, "He's so OCD." When used in this manner, the term is meant to describe someone who has to have things be a certain way, whether or not the person has a clinical diagnosis of OCD.

How about you? Do you avoid touching door handles in public places? Do you always double-check to be sure you locked the door before leaving home? If you answered yes to either of these questions, it does not necessarily mean you have OCD.

Many people have irrational thoughts or carry out unnecessary behaviors to make themselves feel more at ease. For example, some people are superstitious, believing that wearing a lucky hat will help their team win, even though they know their clothing choice has no impact on the outcome of the game. Some people like to be certain that things are turned off, unplugged, or locked, so they will go back to check and make sure. Others are avoiders. They avoid stepping on

A common compulsion among people with OCD is to keep checking that doors and windows are locked. Doing so reduces anxiety, though only temporarily.

cracks in the sidewalk or walking under ladders in order to avert bad luck. These behaviors are seen as quirks, not a clinical disorder.

While people with OCD may have some mannerisms that appear quirky, their thoughts and behaviors are driven by their illness and are not a matter of personal choice. People with OCD have functional differences in the way their brains operate. Says psychiatrist John March, "OCD is considered a neuropsychiatric illness. *Neuro* because OCD is thought to originate in the brain and *psychiatric* because it affects thoughts, feelings, and behavior."[6]

Understanding OCD

OCD is a mental health disorder that affects people of all ages and races. OCD cannot be controlled through willpower. For some people, OCD symptoms arise during childhood, compromising what should be a relatively carefree phase of life. For others, symptoms do not appear until later in life, making it hard to do daily activities and maintain healthy relationships.

Sometimes people say they are obsessed with something they enjoy to a great extent, such as ice cream, yoga, or baseball. But real obsessions cause pain and suffering. Obsessions get stuck in a person's mind and can overpower rational thoughts.

You've no doubt experienced what it is like to get a song stuck in your head. It doesn't take long before the song becomes annoying. Now imagine if that song were playing so frequently inside your head that it blocked out all other thoughts. It would quickly go from irritating to anxiety inducing. Obsessions occur when a person becomes fixated on a thought such as, "I'm certain doorknobs have germs that are going to kill me." The irrational, though real, fear of being killed by germs on doorknobs produces intense and sometimes debilitating anxiety.

Compulsions are the actions a person takes to try to reduce the anxiety produced by an obsession. Compulsions can be physical or mental. Common physical compulsions are washing, checking, repeating, hoarding, and doing things until they feel just right (also referred to as a symmetry compulsion). Physical compulsions are often repeated with great frequency, such as washing one's hands fifteen times in an hour. A mental compulsion consists of words,

Anxious children often seek reassurance from their parents to lessen their anxiety. However, being comforted in this way can strengthen the obsessive-compulsive cycle.

thoughts, or ideas a person says or thinks, such as counting the same thing over and over again in one's head. Compulsions provide only temporary relief from anxiety, so people repeat compulsions over and over. Carrying out compulsive routines, whether mental or physical, can take hours out of a person's day and can interfere with normal functioning, productivity, and interpersonal relationships.

Another way compulsions are counterproductive is that they deceive the person with OCD by making a false connection between thoughts or behaviors and a given result. For example, a person might believe that repeating the Lord's Prayer five times (a mental compulsion) will prevent a flood from happening. After saying the prayers, the flood does not happen, and the person thinks the ritual worked. In reality, there never was any risk of a flood. The brain experiences a false sense of security through the erroneous impression that the ritual worked.

Because OCD sufferers typically struggle with doubt, they feel the need for frequent reassurance. Over time, a given compulsion needs to be replaced with one that is even more elaborate. The person who needed to say the Lord's Prayer five times to avert the flood now finds no relief until she says it ten times.

The OCD Trap

The process of negative reinforcement is what drives the obsessive-compulsive cycle. Negative reinforcement means that any behavior that minimizes or eliminates an unwanted feeling is likely to be repeated. For example, if an anxious child expresses an irrational worry that her parents will die in an airplane crash, seeking and receiving reassurance from the parents will only make it more likely that she will need comfort from them in the future. Because sharing this fear with her parents temporarily lessened her anxiety, she is likely to go back to them whenever her fear comes to mind, often in ever-shortening intervals. If they are unavailable to comfort her, she cannot carry out the ritual that normally brings relief, and her anxiety will heighten.

Clinical psychologist Charles Elliott describes the intense power of negative reinforcement with the example of excessive hand washing to avoid germs: "They engage in a compulsion in order to reduce their worry or distress. . . . The compulsion briefly reduces their distress, but it also powerfully reinforces the obsessional worry that led to the compulsion. An ever worsening cycle ensues. Sometimes these folks gradually increase their hand washing to the point that they do it for hours every day."[7]

An eight-year-old boy explains what living with OCD is like for him. "I feel so stupid when I have to make my footsteps perfectly even and count each one. I can't hold a conversation with my friends, and if I mess up counting, I have to go back and start over. I hate having to pretend I dropped something or make up a lie about why I need to go back to that tree and start walking again—but if I don't go back, somebody could get hurt in my family and that would be the worst."[8]

> "They engage in a compulsion in order to reduce their worry or distress. . . . The compulsion briefly reduces their distress, but it also powerfully reinforces the obsessional worry that led to the compulsion. An ever worsening cycle ensues."[7]
>
> —Charles Elliott, clinical psychologist

This boy described himself as feeling stupid—a common belief among many with OCD. Often their incessant thoughts are not rational. So why, then, would someone be caught in the grip of these thoughts? It is not for lack of intelligence. "Children with OCD are not 'crazy,'" explains March. "[They] typically are quite insightful and . . . tend to be of average or greater intelligence."[9]

Irrational fear is often at the root of obsessions. As with the boy feeling he had to count his footsteps to keep his family from being hurt, many people with OCD believe acting out their compulsions is what protects themselves and others from harm. For example, a girl might think cleaning her room is what keeps her family's house from

An obsession with cleanliness can result in someone spending hours each day washing her hands. This can also extend to repeatedly showering or washing personal possessions.

catching on fire. The fear of having a fire is so distressing that she becomes compulsive about keeping her room immaculate.

Obsessions are often scary and frequently play on what-if scenarios, such as, What if I didn't lock the door and someone breaks in and kills my family? The girl who cleans to save her family from a fire knows her thoughts are illogical, but she can't make them stop. Some people with OCD believe they are going crazy.

Anxiety and Fear

When a person is trapped in the OCD cycle, every attempt to make the obsession stop inadvertently brings more attention to the problem. The more he or she tries to dismiss the thought, the louder and more intrusive the thought becomes. The brain then sends warnings in the form of anxiety. This is the body's distress signal, letting the person know something is wrong or something bad is about to happen.

Anxiety and fear are natural reactions our bodies experience as a means to protect us. When we feel anxious or fearful, our brains send signals to our bodies, alerting us to potential harm or danger. Imagine being in a parking garage late at night and hearing footsteps rapidly approaching from behind. Does your heart begin to race? Does your stomach feel queasy? Are your muscles tense? These physical indicators are your body's way of making you aware of your surroundings. It's telling you to pay attention, as there could be something harmful heading your way.

It is normal to experience some level of anxiety when facing a new or unfamiliar situation. For example, a child moving to a different state naturally wonders whether she will make friends at her new school. Someone starting his first job after college might worry whether he is up to the challenge. Studies indicate that people with OCD have a lower tolerance for uncertainty compared with people overall. When their anxiety overcomes them in the form of obsessive thoughts, people with OCD either perform a ritual to lessen their anxiety or find ways to avoid the distressing thoughts. Avoidance, like compulsions, perpetuates the problems associated with OCD.

It is natural to want to avoid something that causes fear. If a person fears heights, she will likely avoid roller coasters and rock climbing. But being afraid of something that is an essential part of daily life creates complications. For example, if someone with OCD fears contamination, he may refuse food someone else has touched, perhaps preparing all of his own food instead and making excuses for not wanting to eat out. If the fear is further indulged, the obsession with contamination may lead him to avoid buying produce from the store because a grocery clerk handled it. Over time, avoidance heightens the fear, giving it more power.

Learning to recognize fear and anxiety as tools to use in fighting the disorder breaks the OCD cycle. When a person is battling an obsession and feels extremely anxious, it is important for her to recognize that she is not in any real danger. According to psychologist Lee Fitzgibbons, "Think of anxiety as an ice cube. When you pick it up in your hands, it hurts, but as you hold it and it melts, it loses its ability to cause the same kind of pain it first caused. The more you touch the melted water the warmer and less unpleasant it becomes."[10]

> "Think of anxiety as an ice cube. When you pick it up in your hands, it hurts, but as you hold it and it melts, it loses its ability to cause the same kind of pain it first caused. The more you touch the melted water the warmer and less unpleasant it becomes."[10]
>
> —Lee Fitzgibbons, psychologist

Making Sense of OCD

From an outside perspective, it might be hard to understand why a person with OCD behaves in a certain way. Imagine watching someone enter and exit a room over and over, seemingly unable to stop, or witnessing someone wash his hands so often they bleed. It is hard for an outside observer to find meaning in these types of actions.

Psychiatrist Judith Rapoport says, "I liken [OCD] to a hiccup of the mind; people . . . just can't control it."[11] Hiccups are one of the body's autonomic physical reactions. They do not hurt us, but they can sometimes be bothersome. When they last so long that they become uncomfortable, we have techniques to try to get rid of them. Just like a physical hiccup, OCD functions like a mental hiccup in which the brain locks into a certain way of thinking and responding.

In OCD, the part of the brain that filters information does not work properly. Using a computer analogy, a spam filter siphons off messages that are not worth receiving. In the same way, most people have a mental filter that allows them to ignore the brain's "junk mail." People with OCD have trouble distinguishing input that should be received and acted upon from that which should be ignored. This can prompt persistent associations between thoughts and certain actions, causing a person to repeat these actions over and over whenever the thoughts arise. Susie, an eleven-year-old-girl with OCD, has an obsession with cleanliness. She says, "OCD made me wash my hands whenever I would touch something that felt dirty or germy. At the beginning, I thought OCD was something I had to do to keep safe because my little brother had leukemia and we all had to wash our hands a lot, but I realized real fast [my washing] was more than what other kids did."[12] Before long, Susie was washing her hands fifty times a day.

Similar to many people with OCD, Susie's initial reason for her frequent hand washing made perfect sense, but her OCD took her pursuit of cleanliness to an unreasonable level. It's easy to see the connection Susie made between her obsession (cleanliness) and her compulsion (hand washing). But sometimes the relationship between an obsession and its accompanying compulsion is much more obscure. For example, a ten-year-old girl who was afraid of monsters

Howie Mandel

Actor and comedian Howie Mandel, host of the former NBC game show *Deal or No Deal*, speaks openly about having OCD and attention deficit hyperactivity disorder (ADHD). Mandel was not diagnosed until he was an adult. Until then, he wasn't aware that these disorders existed. Mandel's obsession is contamination. He famously gave contestants fist bumps instead of shaking hands in greeting. In a CNN interview, Mandel recalled having one of his shoelaces come untied at school. Mandel didn't want to touch the shoelace because it had touched the ground. He avoided it by walking around all day with a limp so his shoe wouldn't come off. The other kids made fun of him for not knowing how to tie his shoes. Mandel said, "I didn't want to say I do know how to tie my shoes because then I'd have to touch [my shoelace]."[1] Mandel believes the way to make the world a better place is to help everyone be healthier mentally. "We take care of our dental health," he said. "We don't take care of our mental health."[2]

1. Quoted in Jessica Haddad, Eric M. Strauss, and David Muir, "Germs: 'No Deal' for Host Howie Mandel," *ABC News*, November 24, 2009. www.abcnews.go.com.

2. Quoted in Elizabeth Landau, "Howie Mandel: 'We Don't Take Care of Our Mental Health,'" *CNN*, February 1, 2014. www.cnn.com.

developed a specific method for keeping them away. Her doctor explained: "Every time she went into a room, she would have to step in and out twice—one time with her right foot first to let in the good, a second time with her left foot to take out the bad."[13]

The rules and limitations for those living out their OCD compulsions are often detailed and sometimes exhausting. People get tired trying to perform all the actions that the disorder demands. Often the compulsions change and become more extensive. Any relief felt from performing the compulsion—albeit temporary—reinforces the obsession and worsens the condition.

What Does OCD Feel Like?

People with OCD often struggle when they try to explain what it is like living with the disorder. "Many [children] describe OCD as some other voice that sounds sort of believable but has a mind of its own and tells them to think and do things they don't want to. They feel as if someone has taken over their mind," says psychologist Tamar Chansky.[14]

One of the distinguishing characteristics that separates people who have the disorder from those who don't is the ability to distinguish a true threat from a minor concern. For example, if a student without OCD hears someone sneeze in the cafeteria, he may wonder if he will get sick. The thought is fleeting, and the student proceeds to eat his lunch without further concern. At that same moment, another student who has OCD may hear the sneeze and wonder the same thing, except she cannot go on eating her lunch. It's as if she can feel the germs on her plate.

People with OCD are likely to believe their thoughts are in some way a premonition. If a person with OCD is preparing to drive his car, the thought might cross his mind that he could run someone over. That thought can go from, "What if I run someone over?" to "I am going to run someone over." He feels this concern so deeply that it

> "Many [children] describe OCD as some other voice that sounds sort of believable but has a mind of its own and tells them to think and do things they don't want to. They feel as if someone has taken over their mind."[14]
>
> —Tamar Chansky, psychologist

Driving can be very stressful for people with OCD. They may fear causing an accident and injuring someone.

becomes his reality. At that point, he has a choice to make. He can either face the fear by getting behind the wheel and driving, or he can avoid the fear.

Avoidance is a common coping mechanism for those with OCD. Some people try to suppress their thoughts and think about pleasant things that do not cause them anguish. But ironically, the more the man who fears running someone over tries not to think about it, the more likely his thoughts will get stuck on that fear. Mental avoidance requires a conscious effort, so the unwanted thought ends up getting more attention, not less. Behavioral avoidance involves avoiding actions that cause one fear or discomfort; in this example, the man might take the bus or ask a friend for a ride. By avoiding driving, the worried driver tries to prevent a bad outcome, but in doing so, he doesn't allow himself the chance to disprove his fears and feelings about driving. The longer he goes without driving, the more real and scary the obsessive thoughts become.

OCD Incidence

Twenty-five years ago, obsessive-compulsive disorder was thought to be rare. Today, OCD is recognized as one of the most common mental illnesses, affecting about one in every forty people in the United States. About half a million children in the United States suffer from OCD. That means about one in 200 children has the disorder—about the same number of kids who have diabetes. In an average-sized elementary school, four or five children likely have OCD. In a large high school, there may be as many as twenty students with OCD.

Studies show OCD has genetic links. People who have first-degree relatives with OCD (such as a parent, sibling, or child) are more likely to develop the disorder themselves. This is especially true if the relative showed signs of the disorder as a child or teenager.

Boys tend to display symptoms of OCD earlier than girls. Most adults who have OCD recall first experiencing symptoms in their youth. While OCD typically develops during the early adolescent years or late teen/early adult years, there are documented cases of OCD in patients as young as three years old.

Worldwide, the prevalence of OCD seems to mirror that of the United States at approximately 2 percent of the population. Says psychiatrist John March, "The chance of having OCD appears to be remarkably similar all over the world, which is one of the characteristics of a brain disorder. So far as we can tell, an Italian German American child who lives in North Carolina is just as likely to have OCD as his Asian American bunkmate in summer camp who hails from Oregon."[15]

Chapter 2

OCD SYMPTOMS AND DIAGNOSIS

The specific cause of OCD is unknown, but medical professionals theorize that the brains of people with OCD may work differently than those of people without the disorder. Some scientists believe OCD results from a faulty communication loop among various parts of the brain. The orbitofrontal cortex is the part of the brain where thoughts and emotions are processed. It comes into play in decision-making and impulse control. The caudate nucleus is located in the center of the brain. It regulates how learning occurs and plays a vital role in storing and retrieving memories. The thalamus, also located in the center of the brain, serves as a relay station, receiving

The Caudate Nucleus and OCD

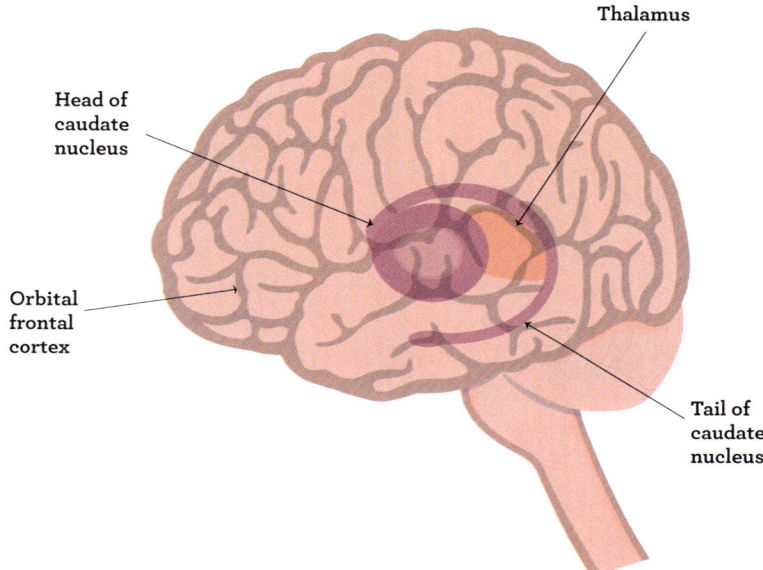

Scientists believe faulty operation of the brain's caudate nucleus is related to OCD. It may cause people with OCD to experience a continuing sense of alarm.

signals from various portions of the brain and directing them to where they belong. The caudate nucleus sits between the orbitofrontal cortex and the thalamus, regulating the messages that are sent back and forth between them.

When the thalamus receives a message that something worrisome is present, it sends a signal to the orbitofrontal cortex by way of the caudate nucleus. A person without OCD has the ability to interpret the thought in a rational manner. However, the person with OCD perceives the message as a threat because, as some researchers hypothesize, the caudate nucleus is in some way damaged and fails to stop the alarm signals sent by the thalamus. The result is that the person continues to perceive a threat is present.

For example, a girl who has developed an obsession with cleanliness may notice dirt on her hands. Her orbitofrontal cortex takes in this information and sends a signal to the thalamus that something is not right. Even though she washes her hands to remove the dirt, her thalamus locks in on the perception that dirt is still present, causing her to wash her hands repeatedly. She continues to experience anxiety despite her hands being objectively clean.

When someone is having OCD symptoms, psychiatrist Jeffrey Schwartz refers to this condition as "brain lock." He likens the brain of a person without OCD to an automatic transmission in a car. In contrast, the brain of a person with OCD operates with more of a manual transmission—one that is sticky and difficult to shift.

In large part, the metabolism of the brain is regulated by chemicals that allow signals to pass from nerve cell to nerve cell. These chemicals are known as neurotransmitters. Serotonin is a neurotransmitter that converses with all parts of our bodies through our cells. It has many functions throughout the body, including helping with digestion and sleep, stabilizing moods, and managing anxiety. Although scientists have yet to determine the cause of OCD, they have discovered that low levels of serotonin are associated with the presence of OCD symptoms and with depression. Depression commonly co-occurs with OCD. It is still unknown if low levels of serotonin cause depression or if depression lowers levels of serotonin. Most medications that are used to treat OCD are antidepressants that boost serotonin levels.

Risk Factors

In addition to having a known genetic link, various factors related to pregnancy and childbirth may be associated with OCD. According to child psychiatry professor James Leckman of Yale University, "There is a fairly strong indication that for some individuals with OCD there is risk that gets started very early in development, even during the prenatal period."[16] Leckman notes that nearly 50 percent of those in a Swedish study who developed OCD had one of the identified risk factors, including premature birth, cesarean birth, breech delivery, abnormally large or small birth weight, or maternal smoking during pregnancy. Having several of these conditions increases a person's likelihood of developing OCD.

> "There is a fairly strong indication that for some individuals with OCD there is risk that gets started very early in development, even during the prenatal period."[16]
>
> —James Leckman, child psychiatry professor

Certain life events are associated with an increased risk for OCD, too. People who have experienced physical and sexual abuse and other traumatic events may have an increased likelihood of developing the disorder. Some research indicates that distressing and life-changing events can spark OCD behaviors in those who are genetically predisposed to the disorder. Further research and more conclusive evidence are needed before a link with trauma can be established.

While stress alone does not cause OCD, it can cause a flare-up in someone who has OCD or is anxious in other ways. According to

PANDAS and PANS

Doctors are studying cases in which children who had strep throat developed a sudden onset of OCD. This is referred to as the PANDAS theory. PANDAS stands for pediatric autoimmune neuropsychiatric disorders associated with streptococcal infections. Clinicians believe the antibodies children produce to fight the strep throat infection damage the brain. Fitzgibbons explains, "PANDAS-related OCD typically has a sudden and severe onset. Often, other neuropsychiatric symptoms surface or worsen at the time the OCD symptoms begin." Some of the neuropsychiatric symptoms that may co-occur include tics, heightened sensory sensitivity, fidgeting, handwriting changes, or loss of math skills. Personality changes can include hyperactivity, irritability, impulsivity, poor attention span, or separation anxiety.

Like PANDAS, the PANS hypothesis refers to children who experience a sudden onset of symptoms of OCD or eating disorders that include self-restricting of food. PANS is short for pediatric acute-onset neuropsychiatric syndrome. The quick, sometimes overnight development separates this illness from a typical OCD diagnosis or eating disorder. The child diagnosed with PANS might demonstrate feelings of depression, anxiety, and irritability, and he or she may have trouble focusing. According to PANS theory, these sudden behavioral and mental changes are caused by infection, metabolic disturbances, and other inflammatory reactions.

The debate regarding PANDAS and PANS is ongoing. Some argue there is not enough evidence to prove that an infectious illness can cause such pronounced behavioral changes. Others argue that the swift changes in behavior observed in PANDAS and PANS cases can be logically explained by an inflammatory process.

Lee Fitzgibbons and Cherlene Pedrick, *Helping Your Child with OCD*. Oakland: New Harbinger, 2003, p 14.

the Anxiety and Depression Association of America, "A stress trigger or trauma may precipitate symptoms [of OCD].... And if OCD symptoms are already present, stress can worsen them."[17]

According to studies, the majority of adults in the United States who suffer from OCD have suffered from some other type of mental health disorder at some point in their life. When two or more disorders occur within the same person, the conditions are said to be comorbid disorders. Common comorbid disorders that exist alongside OCD are anxiety disorders, depression, tic disorders, and substance abuse. Comorbidity affects both disorders and has the potential to make both disorders worse.

The Nature of Obsessions

True obsessions in the psychiatric sense are deep, controlling, often frightening, and difficult to overcome. People with OCD may experience repeated thoughts they are unable to turn off. Many are embarrassed and try to keep their obsessions secret.

Jake, a sixteen-year-old student with an above-average IQ, had OCD and believed he was losing his intelligence. He developed a series of rituals to prevent his brain cells from dying. These included opening his school locker while standing on one foot, putting his clothing on in a certain order, and touching each corner of a room before exiting the room. When Jake was unable to complete his SAT test because of his constant erasing and redoing, his parents took him to see psychiatrist Harold Koplewicz. Koplewicz discovered Jake had been having problems with OCD since he was ten years old. Said Koplewicz, "It is not unusual for parents to be kept in the dark about OCD. Many children, realizing that their symptoms

> "It is not unusual for parents to be kept in the dark about OCD. Many children, realizing that their symptoms make no sense and feeling a sense of shame about them, keep their symptoms secret."[18]
>
> —Harold Koplewicz, psychiatrist

make no sense and feeling a sense of shame about them, keep their symptoms secret."[18]

Obsessions induce anxiety because they are so invasive and recurrent. Chansky says an OCD brain is like a net catching thoughts. "When you've got OCD, your net is of finer mesh on a longer pole. It dredges up all sorts of thoughts other people's nets miss. You have not chosen those thoughts so you are not responsible for them. They just happen."[19] The person with OCD can't stop herself from thinking unwanted thoughts, so she feels distress and becomes anxious. To combat her anxiety, she establishes rituals, hoping to suppress the thoughts from occurring again.

OCD shares some similarities with a condition known as generalized anxiety disorder, or GAD. People with GAD don't feel in control of their worry just as people with OCD don't feel in control of their thoughts. A person with GAD constantly worries about ordinary things but in the extreme. For example, he may wonder, "What if I fail my test?" This is a normal concern, but the person with GAD spins it out of proportion. The thought of "What if I fail my test?" becomes "I won't get into college."

People with OCD and GAD may have concerns about the same things, but for people with OCD, the anticipated consequences are often not logically tied to the precipitating event. The person with OCD who is worried about failing a test may believe someone he loves will get hurt if he fails.

Common Obsessions

The most common obsession is the fear of touching something contaminated. Furniture, door handles, pencils, food, even a person's

People with OCD experience uncertainty more often than people without the condition. Constant rechecking can make it difficult for students to take tests.

own clothing—anything that could be viewed as unclean becomes the focus of the obsession. The person fears that by coming into contact with germs, he or she could get sick or could die.

Another common obsession is the fear of hurting oneself or others. This obsession is often dealt with through avoidance. If indulged, the obsession can prevent a person from driving, riding a bicycle, using knives, or performing other actions he believes could harm himself or others. Sometimes this person also has an unrealistic fear of harming animals and insects.

A man who was obsessed with the thought of hurting someone with his car drove back and forth on the same road repeatedly until he finally got out of his car and combed the side of the road looking for evidence that he had hit someone. He says, "The pain is a terrible guilt that I have committed an unthinkable, negligent act. At one level I know this is ridiculous, but there's a terrible pain in my stomach telling me something quite different."[20]

The need for symmetry, another common obsession, is a fixation on order, exactness, and alignment. It may compel a person to line up his shoes in his closet and evenly hang his clothes in the same direction. An obsession with symmetry can also be applied to a person's body. A fifteen-year old boy noted, "My OCD tells me I have to make my nails perfectly even or it doesn't feel right. Same with my feet. I have to shake my legs evenly on both sides; if I don't do it evenly or if I lose count, I have to start all over. I could spend a whole class period shaking my legs. . . . It's just that it won't feel right unless it's even."[21]

> "My OCD tells me I have to make my nails perfectly even or it doesn't feel right. Same with my feet. I have to shake my legs evenly on both sides; if I don't do it evenly or if I lose count, I have to start all over."[21]
>
> —fifteen-year-old boy with OCD

Being unsure or doubting is an obsession that makes people constantly second-guess themselves. Such a person is always wondering if she did or did not do something. Did she turn off the stove, lock the door, turn in her work, or leave the window open? Even when she gives in to the obsession and checks, she is still full of doubts. Checking can occur numerous times until she is satisfied or her ritual is interrupted.

Morgan, a college student with OCD, explains her obsession with doubting. "It starts as a whisper, a little hint or suggestion to repeat a behavior." She describes feeling compelled to reread a sentence. Then she feels the need to reread a paragraph. The pattern continues until she finds herself reading something over and over again. She says, "Before you even realize it has happened and have the chance to stop it, OCD has grown into a raging monster that treats you like a puppet."[22]

A person who believes he needs to do something a certain number of times to avoid harm may have an obsession with numbers. He might compulsively count the steps he takes, the sentences he reads, or the letters in the words he hears. Others may have numbers they feel are unlucky or bad and will avoid these numbers at all costs. It is difficult for a person to pay attention to other thoughts if he is always counting or thinking about numbers.

A person with a religious obsession, also referred to as scrupulosity, may worry that he is sinning or is a bad person. He obsesses over right and wrong and often feels the compulsive need to pray unceasingly or repetitiously. He may pray to save the people around him from danger. People with this obsession may feel the need to constantly confess their thoughts and actions.

Diane, a woman affected with scrupulosity, began withdrawing from her friends and family when her symptoms first showed up at age twenty-five. Once an active member of her church, she began to feel like a hypocrite. She said, "I was scared to look at people. I thought I was offending them by inappropriately glancing at them, and I constantly prayed for forgiveness."[23] People with this obsession

Some people with OCD feel a compulsion to hoard items. For some, the prospect of discarding these items can produce extreme anxiety.

use prayer as a compulsion to counteract the thoughts they perceive as bad.

Hoarding is a both an obsession and a compulsion that goes beyond inner turmoil in one's thoughts. The compelling need to accumulate things has a dramatic effect on the hoarder and the people who live with him or her. The obsession is the need to save or purchase things. The compulsion is the act of collecting or hoarding the items.

While hoarding can be a separate mental disorder from OCD, many mental health professionals also view it as an OCD subtype. Hoarders who have OCD find the hoarding obsession distressing and usually don't feel an attachment to the things they collect or view them as valuable. The target of their hoarding impulse doesn't always make sense, as some people even collect garbage.

As many as one-quarter of adults with OCD obsess over unwanted sexual thoughts. They might doubt or obsess over their sexuality or sexual orientation. Or they obsess over perverse thoughts or impulses, even including incest, pedophilia, or sexual violence. People who suffer from this obsession seldom act on it and often experience shame and self-loathing.

Compulsions

Compulsions coerce a person into doing something he doesn't want to do in a way that interferes with the things he'd rather be doing. When he submits to his ritual he experiences a moment of reprieve from his anxiety. But this also negatively reinforces his compulsion. Compulsions can feel inescapable. For example, think about the number seven. Now, imagine if you couldn't stop thinking about the number seven. Perhaps you have to brush your teeth seven times, comb your hair seven times, and chew each bite of food exactly seven times. The need to do everything seven times makes it almost impossible to accomplish what you need to do throughout the day. You want to stop. You don't want to reread a page seven times, but in order to make the feeling to go away, you do it.

Unlike obsessive thoughts that can't be repressed, compulsions can be resisted to a certain degree or delayed for a period of time.

OC SPECTRUM DISORDERS

OC Spectrum Disorders	What Is It?	Similarities to OCD	Differences from OCD
Body Focused Repetitive Behaviors (BFRBs) *Trichotillomania* (TTM) or 'trich' *Dermatillomania*, or excoriation	People with TTM compulsively pull their hair out. Dermatillomania is the act of picking one's skin to the point of damage.	People with BFRBs do their repetitive behaviors in response to feeling uncomfortable. They feel good in the moment when they pick their skin or pull their hair out.	People with OCD are trying to get away from negative feelings. They give into their urges to avoid feeling anxious.
Body Dysmorphic Disorder (BDD)	People with BDD are fixated on their looks. They identify a part of their body they perceive to be flawed. Obsession with the perceived flaw consumes their thoughts.	People with OCD and BDD engage in repetitive checking. Both experience unrealistic thoughts or obsessions. Both perform compulsions to avoid negative thoughts.	Unlike people with BDD, people with OCD don't typically focus on the way they look.
Hoarding Disorder (HD)	People with HD have great difficulty getting rid of things even if the items possess no value. They receive pleasure from keeping their hoards. Their homes can become so cluttered that they are unsafe and unhygienic.	People with HD and people with OCD who have a hoarding obsession and/or compulsion collect things and have trouble throwing things away.	Unlike people with HD, people with OCD do not want to engage in compulsive behavior, do not receive pleasure from hoarding, and have no attachment to hoarded items.

Neuropsychiatric conditions that share some characteristics with OCD are known as OC spectrum disorders. Therapists modify their treatments to address clients' specific needs.

If a person with OCD fears ridicule when engaging in a compulsion, she may be able to temporarily suspend her ritual. For instance, if a student feels the need to wash her hands repeatedly at school but worries her friends will think she is weird, she may be able to avoid washing until she gets home. Chansky explains, "Children have some ability to delay rituals, but that doesn't mean the moment is forgotten. . . . The compulsions are still going to happen; they just pay the penalty later."[24]

Diagnosing OCD

In the United States, most clinicians use the *Diagnostic and Statistical Manual of Mental Health Disorders* (*DSM-5*) to diagnose mental illnesses. *DSM-5* is the 2013 edition of the manual, which was first published in 1952. This tool provides official definitions and criteria for diagnosing mental disorders and dysfunctions. According to the *DSM-5*, an OCD diagnosis is warranted when:

- A person exhibits obsessions and/or compulsions.
- Obsessions and compulsions take up more than one hour per day and cause significant distress.
- The obsessive-compulsive symptoms are not caused by the use of drugs or by another medical condition.
- The symptoms are not due to another mental disorder. (There are many disorders that mask themselves or co-occur with OCD.)

A person experiencing these symptoms would need to seek professional help in order to be diagnosed with OCD. People often start with their own family doctor or pediatrician. The Stanford University School of Medicine suggests, "Patients may not reveal embarrassing symptoms or symptoms that they believe may suggest they are 'crazy' until a trusting therapeutic relationship has been established."[25] The International OCD Foundation (IOCDF) is a nonprofit organization that provides a wealth of information for anyone needing assistance finding the right therapist. It recommends interviewing potential therapists before beginning treatment. It is important that the patient feels comfortable with her doctor as she will surely be asked to step out of her comfort zone as she progresses in her therapy.

OCD specialist Lee Fitzgibbons explains the importance of getting help early on when OCD symptoms become evident in childhood. "OCD symptoms wax and wane, [so] it's possible your child will have periods during which they struggle with their symptoms and also experience periods where they are relatively symptom-free. What we do know is that many adults with OCD report an onset in childhood with a gradually worsening course until they received treatment. These adults say that they wish their problem had been identified and addressed sooner."[26]

For adults who did not experience OCD symptoms in childhood, it can be a confusing journey to identify and sort out OCD symptoms when they become evident. As often happens with unwanted medical conditions, many adults ignore or

> "What we do know is that many adults with OCD report an onset in childhood with a gradually worsening course until they received treatment. These adults say that they wish their problem had been identified and addressed sooner."[26]
>
> —Lee Fitzgibbons, OCD specialist

downplay their symptoms, hoping they will go away. A group of German researchers wanted to know why so many adults delayed treatment. They examined a group of 40 patients with OCD. On average, those patients waited six and a half years from initial onset of symptoms before seeking professional help. The researchers note that "approximately 40% of the participants reported fear of stigmatization and discrimination as a major reason for the delay in the first attempt at seeking help."[27]

    A clinician will likely administer tests to help with the diagnosis. A commonly used test that systematically screens adults and teens for OCD is the Yale-Brown Obsessive Compulsive Scale (Y-BOCS). There is also a Children's Yale-Brown Obsessive Compulsive Scale (CY-BOCS). There are several online tests that claim they can tell if a person has OCD. These tests can't be validated as accurate. Self-diagnosis is unreliable, and many signs and symptoms can mask themselves as something else or suggest a variety of conditions. An online test can be misleading and is in no way a substitute for seeking the opinion of a qualified professional such as a psychologist, psychiatrist, or other trained therapist.

Chapter 3

THE IMPACT OF OCD

When a person has OCD, she cannot take for granted a variety of everyday tasks that many people perform with ease. But OCD not only disrupts the life of the person with the disorder, it also affects the entire family. A daughter might take long or very frequent showers, which take time, raise water bills, and monopolize a family bathroom. Fearing contamination, she might eat meals alone rather than with her family. Or her grades might drop if she cannot complete homework because of compulsive checking and rechecking. A parent might work fewer hours so he can spend more time caring for a daughter with OCD. If the father also has OCD, he might struggle to hold down a job because his time-consuming compulsions prevent him from completing his work.

Family dynamics change when one family member begins displaying signs of OCD. When people with OCD start experiencing symptoms, they often keep their obsessions and compulsions to

Parents are often at a loss to know how to help their child cope with OCD. Seeking expert advice can help.

themselves. If a child shows a new tendency toward secrecy, parents may dismiss it as a sign of growing up. But it could also be a means of hiding a compulsive behavior.

Most often, OCD symptoms emerge during the teen or young adult years. In what can be a turbulent time in any family, tension may increase as parents and children struggle to understand what is going on. Home life that was once calm and orderly can become unpredictable and unpleasant.

Just as children and teens with OCD must learn skills to manage their OCD, their parents must learn coping strategies, too. Many families seek group therapy so they can educate themselves on living with OCD.

Children and Teens Living with OCD

It is not uncommon for children with OCD to be up late at night with obsessive thoughts or rituals long after everyone else has gone to sleep. Parents may not be aware that their son or daughter is getting only a few hours of sleep. A thirteen-year-old engaged in some very time-consuming bedtime rituals. Her therapist explains,

> *Lining up all her stuffed animals in her room, she has to say good night to each one, give each one a kiss, make sure they don't fall over, and look them in the eyes. When that is done, she starts with her prayers, which must include every family member, friend, animal, and child she has seen on the news or heard about; if she forgets someone, she has to start over because it wasn't a good prayer, it had a mistake in it. On a good night, she can get the ritual done in 45 minutes; on bad nights, she is up most of the night, alternating between trying to get the ritual right and worrying about the terrible harm she may have done by not doing it perfectly.*[28]

Another girl, age sixteen, describes what nights are like for her: "I try to dodge [OCD] when I'm going to sleep at night, I try to trick it that I'm asleep, but I just crack my eyes, it's there waiting for me: 'You have to deal with me—think about horror, think about Bosnia.' And then it's over. I'm up for hours."[29]

Mornings are often stressful for people with OCD. Family members may get impatient if the person with OCD slows down the process of getting ready to go by performing a ritual or acting on a compulsion. Often, as the person with OCD feels more pressure, his stress increases, thus strengthening the urge to perform more compulsions.

Family schedules can be upset when a child carries out compulsions at inconvenient times. Parents may feel stressed as a result.

Parents and OCD

When parents discover that a child has OCD, two different reactions are common. Some parents are willing to do almost anything to ease their child's pain. Others react out of anger and impatience, not understanding the challenges of the disorder.

Many parents unwittingly reinforce a child's OCD by performing rituals for him. One child psychiatrist says, "A ten-year-old boy with a cleanliness obsession takes several showers a day. His mother stands outside the door and hands in fresh towels to the boy, sometimes as many as half a dozen per shower."[30] Perhaps the mother thought she was speeding things along by helping her son. However good her intentions were, when parents assist a child with his compulsions, they are hurting him instead of helping him.

A parent might have several reasons for indulging a child's compulsions. First, she might think that by helping him, she can relieve some of his stress. It's difficult for anyone to see someone they love in pain. Second, she might participate in her child's rituals out of growing frustration. OCD is exhausting for the child with the disorder as well as for parents. Third, a parent is sometimes embarrassed by her child's OCD and wants to keep it hidden. She might give in to her child's obsessions to avoid a meltdown. To an outsider, OCD might look more like a temper tantrum than a disorder. The parent might hope to avoid public judgment or shaming.

Parents can also make matters worse by choosing avoidance. It may be easier to avoid going places such as a restaurant or a store than to deal with a child's OCD. Some parents might avoid allowing visitors in their homes because it is too difficult to explain the child's behavior. Others might avoid going on vacation because it would be exhausting to accommodate their child's rituals in a new setting.

OCD can wreak havoc on a marriage, as uncertainty and stress arise when troubling behaviors emerge. Parents may find themselves disagreeing with each other about how to deal with their child's illness. They might begin to resent each other if they become unequal caregivers. Sometimes parents wrongfully blame each other for the OCD. But OCD is no one's fault—not the parents or family members and not the person who has it.

Additional caregiving needs can stress families too. OCD specialist Lee Fitzgibbons says, "The impact on the family can extend to the economic realm. Sometimes parents miss work because of their child's OCD crises. In extreme cases, absenteeism can lead to job loss. Or a parent may decide to stop working in order to be more available to the child. The cost of treatment, both medication and therapy, can drain financial resources further."[31] When a family's finances are negatively affected, the strain can be felt by everyone in the family.

Siblings and OCD

Siblings, in particular, may be negatively affected by their brother's or sister's OCD. Many siblings feel resentment toward their brother or sister with OCD and also toward their parents. They may find it unfair if household rules don't apply to everyone in the same way. For example, a child who obsesses about contamination may be allowed to avoid eating certain foods while the other kids in the family have to eat what they are served. Or a child with a hoarding compulsion may be allowed to keep a cluttered bedroom even though the other siblings have to be neat and tidy. It may be difficult for other kids in the family—especially young siblings—to understand the challenges of the disorder.

Being a brother or sister to someone with OCD can be complicated. Some siblings feel neglected when so much of the

> "The impact on the family can extend to the economic realm. Sometimes parents miss work because of their child's OCD crises. In extreme cases, absenteeism can lead to job loss. . . .The cost of treatment, both medication and therapy, can drain financial resources further."[31]
>
> —Lee Fitzgibbons, OCD specialist

OCD can strain family relationships. Children who have a sibling with OCD may resent the parental attention given to their sibling.

parents' attention is being given to the child with OCD. The mother of two sons, one with OCD and one who does not have the condition, said,

> *Siblings are OCD's often overlooked victims. They are witness to, and often participant in, the tumult. Often, they stand helplessly by as their siblings struggle through painful rituals. They get dragged along to therapy appointments. They see activities missed. They experience the conflict. They can be targets of their sibling's compulsions or the object of their obsessions. They watch Mom and Dad in angst and sometimes they feel completely overlooked.*[32]

Siblings may begin acting out as a means to get attention. Or the opposite may be true and they may feel the need to be perfect to make life easier for their parents. Some might find their sibling's behavior embarrassing and therefore avoid being seen with their sibling. When they are home, they may retreat to their bedroom, preferring to be alone. Siblings might also have conflicted feelings, having a sense of protective love at the same time as wanting nothing to do with their brother or sister.

    For siblings and parents alike, having a family member with OCD means facing a lot of uncertainty about how best to help their loved one. They want to make life easier for their family member, yet they don't want to feed compulsions and allow them to take over family life. Denise Egan Stack, a licensed mental health counselor, says, "Family members . . . come to realize that their accommodation behaviors are usually done with resentment, hostility, and criticism, which increase emotional upset instead of decreasing it."[33] Also, by focusing so much attention on their loved one, family members may neglect their own personal needs, which can breed negativity over time. Mental health experts recommend therapy for family members who are impacted by OCD.

Academic Concerns

For the student with OCD, school presents many challenges. Understandably, a student will have difficulty focusing on her lessons if she is distracted by a compulsion such as counting or checking. Her distractions may lead to academic difficulties, which can then affect self-esteem. Tests, in particular, can bring overwhelming anxiety for students who want to do well academically but experience a lot of

Retrain the Brain

Jeffrey Schwartz, a psychiatrist at the UCLA School of Medicine, is a leading expert in the field of OCD research. He and his research team thought if people could see their OCD as a biochemical imbalance in the brain, they might look at their urges differently and be more inclined to resist them. Perhaps they would be able to separate themselves from their OCD.

He and research partner Lew Baxter studied a group of people diagnosed with OCD. They injected a glucose-like substance into their patients and monitored brain activity while the patients worked. They used high-tech equipment that essentially took pictures of their brains. What Schwartz discovered changed the way patients saw themselves and their disorder.

The pictures indicated that the brains of those with OCD function differently from those not affected by the disorder. Schwartz said, "The use of energy is consistently higher than is normal in the orbital cortex—the underside of the front of the brain. Thus, the orbital cortex is, in essence, working overtime, literally heating up." His hope was to inspire people with OCD to realize that their disorder had an identifiable cause related to brain function. Once realizing that it was not their fault, he wanted to help them retrain their brain through the use of behavioral therapy. However, this research remains inconclusive and other studies have yielded opposite results.

Jeffrey M. Schwartz and Beverly Beyette, *Brain Lock*. New York: Harper Perennial, 2016, p. xlvi.

---

mental static because of their obsessions. Outside the classroom, some students are too exhausted by indulging their compulsions to participate in extracurricular activities, or they avoid such activities because they involve something that will increase their anxiety. For example, a student who is obsessed with cleanliness might not want to share sports equipment or play a team sport where many hands touch a ball.

Each child or teen with OCD must make the personal decision whether to tell school staff about his or her disorder. If staff members

Students with OCD may have difficulty focusing on their studies when their minds are preoccupied with obsessions. Asking teachers for accommodations may help.

are aware of the child's disorder, they can assist the student if she has difficulties or is mistreated by other students. Many teachers are willing to make accommodations for a student with OCD. For instance, a teacher may reduce the amount of homework or grant extra time for completing tasks. Students might be given a quiet place to take tests or be given tests orally instead of in writing. A student with a contamination obsession might receive extra bathroom passes, get to use special utensils, or have a personal chair no one else can sit in. If the OCD is severe enough, the staff and parents may collaborate in writing an individualized education plan (IEP), in which case special accommodations will be formalized.

Jacob, a student with OCD, spent many years in a self-contained special education classroom because he was mistakenly labeled as having behavior problems. With the help of a supportive school staff and his parents, Jacob got an IEP to support his learning needs. He was able to move into general education classes. His mother wrote, "Too often we hear stories of the failure to think of students as individuals with unique needs. Tales of students who are provided services based on their diagnosis, not based on who they are and what will work best for them." She praised the school district for "being collaborative and having an outstanding willingness to think in innovative ways."[34]

Social Concerns

Beyond academic learning, school plays an important part in social development. People form friendships, practice social skills, and learn who they are by interacting with others at school. A student who engages in compulsions may be identified by his peers as different or odd. He may lash out in anger when someone unknowingly interrupts his mental rituals. This can cause embarrassment and increase the student's stress, which, in turn, can trigger OCD symptoms. Says psychiatry professor Eric Storch, "Kids with OCD are really experiencing higher rates of peer problems than other kids." Storch adds, "For a lot of kids [with OCD], peers don't understand what is going on. They are isolated. They are ostracized because it doesn't make sense why they are washing their hands. Why they keep repeating questions."[35]

OCD advocate Janet Singer helped her son Dan overcome such severe OCD that he was unwilling to eat. Singer advises educating students about OCD in an age-appropriate manner when someone in their class has OCD. Says Singer, "Perhaps one of the biggest benefits of educating children is that providing them with information on brain disorders will likely decrease the stigma associated with all types of mental illnesses."[36] Jared Kant, who wrote a book about his experiences with OCD, received a positive reaction when he shared his diagnosis with his friends and explained what it was like to have OCD. He said, "While you might run into some mean-spirited responses, you're also likely to encounter many compassionate ones. True friends will understand your situation and be there for you."[37]

> "For a lot of kids [with OCD], peers don't understand what is going on. They are isolated. They are ostracized because it doesn't make sense why they are washing their hands. Why they keep repeating questions."[35]
>
> —Eric Storch, psychiatry professor

Adults and OCD

Children living with parents who suffer from OCD are often subject to their parents' compulsions. Marla, a woman who always knew she wanted things to be in perfect order, received a phone call reporting that her daughter was crying inconsolably at school. The class had been working on Christmas ornaments, and Marla's daughter knew her ornament would not be allowed on their tree because it didn't

Children and teens with OCD often feel isolated. Peers may see their behaviors as strange and not befriend them.

match the rest of the ornaments. Marla said, "I was crushed that my issue had affected my daughter so strongly. At that young of an age, she knew that I wouldn't allow a nonmatching ornament on the tree."[38]

Kylie, a mother of three, developed a fear of contamination that greatly impacted how she was raising her children. She said, "I was spending up to 16 hours a day locked in a vicious battle of intrusive thoughts, complicated rituals and ever-increasing anxiety. I had become housebound—believing that just by setting foot outside would mean we would catch some deadly disease."[39] Through therapy and medication, Kylie has been able to resume a normal life.

Many adults who've allowed their OCD to go untreated admit to feeling exhausted, stressed, and even suicidal. One woman writes of her OCD this way: "It was beyond terrible . . . hours upon hours would be about wiping, washing, cleaning. Life was shrinking and becoming a battle. All sense of enjoyment lost as everything posed a 'risk.'" She adds, "OCD took 10 years of our marriage, 10 years of both our lives, 10 years of not living as we should have, of fearing almost everything and reaching a place where killing myself honestly was a very real option."[40]

Depression and OCD

More than 60 percent of people diagnosed with OCD also suffer from depression at least once in their lifetime. According to the American Psychiatric Association, "Depression . . . is a common and serious medical illness that negatively affects how you feel, the way you think and how you act. . . . Depression causes feelings of sadness and/or a loss of interest in activities once enjoyed. It can lead to a variety of emotional and physical problems and can decrease a person's ability to function at work and at home."[41]

Studies have found that people with OCD who are also depressed do not respond to therapy as well as people without depression. When a person is battling depression, she might not have the will to participate in

> "Depression . . . is a common and serious medical illness that negatively affects how you feel, the way you think and how you act. Depression causes feelings of sadness and/or a loss of interest in activities once enjoyed."[41]
>
> —American Psychiatric Association

A person with OCD may be sleep deprived if she is repeatedly kept awake by troubling thoughts. Lack of sleep can then lead to other physical problems.

her OCD treatment. For a person suffering from both disorders, it can be best to treat the depression first so the OCD therapy is more likely to be effective.

Physical Effects of OCD

OCD can also cause physical side effects. A person with a washing compulsion may wash her hands so often they become chapped and start bleeding. Someone who stays up at night checking things or performing other rituals can become sleep deprived, which can lead to multiple health issues. The anxiety that comes with OCD may cause headaches, stomachaches, muscle tension, shortness of breath, rapid heartbeat, and/or dizziness.

Some people who suffer from OCD appear to have an eating disorder. They show signs of malnourishment and are underweight. At first appearance, it may look as if they have anorexia nervosa, an eating disorder characterized by the fear of gaining weight. Upon further examination, what appeared to be anorexia may actually be OCD. A young woman's fear of contamination may cause her to not eat. Other reasons for not eating don't have anything to do with contamination. Someone may need to chew her food or count the bites on her plate a certain number of times until it feels right. Or she might be convinced her food contains poison, so she throws it away. She may get stuck reading labels and researching where her food comes from, unable to make a decision about what to purchase. If she has a symmetry obsession, she may not want to disturb the order of her food or upset the organization she has established in her cabinets and refrigerator.

Brian was a thirteen-year-old boy brought to the emergency room because of dehydration. His doctor said, "It all started when he refused to eat Reese's Pieces candies (prominently featured in the movie *E.T.*, Brian's favorite). Brian was preoccupied with the idea that if he ate Reese's Pieces, something terrible would happen to him. The fear of Reese's Pieces led to a fear of peanut butter and then, gradually, to a fear of just about all food."[42] Although the emergency room staff first assumed Brian had anorexia, by probing further, they discerned that OCD was driving Brian's food avoidance. Obtaining a correct diagnosis enabled Brian to receive appropriate treatment for his condition.

… Chapter 4

TREATMENT FOR OCD

Mental health professionals have developed various treatment options to help people with OCD. The goal of treatment is not only to learn how to manage OCD but to learn how to thrive with it.

Cognitive Behavioral Therapy

The brain is a complex organ that has the ability to adapt and change with cognitive behavioral therapy (CBT). CBT is a type of psychotherapy, or talk therapy. When a client meets with a mental health counselor, the therapist helps the patient identify negative or inaccurate thoughts. This awareness enables the client to better understand real-life situations and react to them appropriately. For example, when a woman has an intrusive thought such as, "My hands are covered in germs," she is coached to examine the thought and decide first whether it is true and then whether it requires a response.

Psychotherapy is often a lifeline to a person struggling with OCD. Developing practical ways to deal with obsessions can be very worthwhile.

The point is not to stop the thoughts but to redirect the patient's perception of the thoughts and how she reacts to them.

Psychologist Ben Martin explains, "CBT is a short-term, goal-oriented psychotherapy treatment that takes a hands-on, practical approach to problem-solving."[43] It is both a cognitive (thinking) and behavioral (doing) therapy, because it encourages a patient to think in a new way so she can act in a new way.

There are many advantages to CBT, and numerous patients have found great success using it. The skills learned in CBT can be applied long after therapy ends and can help patients stay on track in managing their OCD.

CBT: The Basics

Cognitive behavioral therapy begins with identifying things in a person's life that are causing him distress. From this list, he and his therapist identify which problems to address first. Then they set goals and make a plan for how to achieve them. The patient will be asked to share his thoughts, feelings, and beliefs about his problems. With the help of his therapist, he will begin recognizing negative thinking or ways that he misinterprets situations. He may be asked to keep a journal to record how he responds physically and mentally to certain situations. In time, he will begin to reshape his thinking by asking himself if his thoughts and beliefs are based on perception or fact. The duration of CBT is different for every person, but it typically lasts an average of ten to twenty sessions. In addition to individual therapy, CBT is offered in group settings, online, and by telephone.

Exposure and Response Prevention (E/RP)

Researchers have found the most effective form of cognitive behavioral therapy for OCD to be exposure and response prevention (E/RP). Basically, this is training the person with OCD to do the opposite of what they would normally want to do. Instead of avoiding an unpleasant thought, the patient is taught to confront it. When the patient feels compelled to do a ritual, he learns through therapy how to refrain from doing so.

E/RP is not easy, as it challenges the patient and deliberately makes her uncomfortable. It requires commitment and hard work. For example, if she has a contamination obsession and a hand-washing compulsion, she may be asked to touch something she perceives as dirty (exposure) and wait to wash her hands (response prevention). With practice, she lengthens the amount of time she waits before washing her hands. Her eventual goal is to no longer feel the need to compulsively wash her hands when faced with this misperception.

The first step in exposure and response prevention is monitoring one's fears. A patient might be asked to track her obsessions and compulsions throughout the day and record the events that trigger her fear. This process of monitoring and recording can take several days. The second step is rating these fears from one to ten, with one being the least scary and ten the scariest. For example, if she has a fear of germs, she might list a fear of using a communal pen as a three, shaking someone's hand as a six, and using a public restroom as a ten. Step three is where she faces her fears. She will deliberately expose herself to her fear until there is a noticeable drop in her anxiety. She might be asked to touch a doorknob and wait until her anxiety subsides. Initially this will cause her distress, but eventually her anxiety will diminish. Gradually the exposures become more intense as, for example, she may be asked to touch more things that have been touched by many hands. E/RP engages the patient in repeated exposure until the behavioral and sensory responses no longer register as fear. Habituation occurs for the patient, which means she no longer feels the same strong response to these events she now encounters frequently. Just as someone who lives next to an airport becomes accustomed to the sound of airplanes taking off, a person with OCD learns to ignore stimuli that once provoked a strong response.

E/RP is done gradually, because it is important for the person with OCD to build success over time. If the therapy starts off too aggressively, the patient is likely to feel overwhelmed, anxious, and discouraged. He or she should find a mental health professional who is trained and qualified to provide this type of treatment. E/RP is usually administered by a psychologist, social worker, or mental health counselor. Typically, patients will visit their therapist's office every week, or more often for more intensive therapy.

If treatment is not administered correctly, it is likely to do more harm than good. The symptoms of many mental disorders look a lot alike, but a patient's treatment should be tailored to his specific condition. E/RP is not effective for all disorders on the obsessive-compulsive spectrum. For example, people with a hoarding disorder may require a different type of therapy from E/RP or other anxiety-based treatments. People with body-focused repetitive behaviors such as skin picking or hair pulling often find habit reversal therapy (HRT) combined with stimulus control to be helpful. They learn to identify when an urge to pick or pull is coming on and immediately start a competing response, such as clenching fists, that will prevent them from picking. Stimulus control means changing the environment to make it more difficult to engage in the picking or pulling behavior, such as wearing a hat to cover the hair.

Medication: Pros and Cons

Many people with OCD use antidepressants to help them function in daily life. They report that medications lessen the intensity of their OCD symptoms. Two classes of drugs are commonly used to treat OCD: serotonin-norepinephrine reuptake inhibitors (SNRIs) and selective serotonin reuptake inhibitors (SSRIs). The difference between the two is that SNRIs affect several neurotransmitters in the brain, while SSRIs target only serotonin.

Medications are widely available with a prescription, and many people find them effective, especially combined with talk therapy. But there are often side effects, including headaches, weight gain, and insomnia. Some medications are expensive, and they may or may not be covered by insurance. In addition, it can take several weeks before patients begin to feel the effects of the medication, prompting some to give up before they've had a chance to see if it works.

Some medications require the patient to taper off their prescriptions gradually or risk worsening their OCD symptoms. A clinical psychologist describes what could happen if someone abruptly stops using amphetamines, one type of drug sometimes used to treat mental disorders: "People can have strong dependency issues with amphetamines. They provide a boost in energy and a state of relative optimism, so when someone's taken off them, it's not unusual to crash. Some patients need rehab to get off of them."[44]

For children as young as three years old, doctors recommend medication over psychotherapy. Cognitive behavioral therapy is not used for treating very young OCD patients. This therapy requires active participation and sophisticated thinking on the part of the patient. Those skills are typically beyond a young child's capabilities. Some parents might be reluctant to give prescription medicines to their children. However, psychiatrist

> "People can have strong dependency issues with amphetamines. They provide a boost in energy and a state of relative optimism, so when someone's taken off them, it's not unusual to crash."[44]
>
> —Clinical psychologist

Harold Koplewicz explains, "[Parents] should be mindful that while there may be negative side effects of medicine, there are also negative effects connected to not taking medication. . . . What we do know is that a child in pain has to have some relief."[45]

Combining Psychotherapy and Medication

Taken together, E/RP and medication are considered the first-line treatment for OCD. About 70 percent of patients find the combination of E/RP and medication to be the most effective treatment for the disorder. E/RP is stressful, and it increases the patient's anxiety at first. One benefit of prescription medicines such as SNRIs and SSRIs is that they help reduce anxiety, making uncomfortable exposure to fears more tolerable.

The downside to this simultaneous treatment is that it can make it difficult to determine which part is or isn't working. If the patient is making progress, is it because of his therapy or his medication? If there is a setback, the same question might be asked. Many people begin with both treatments to help ease their anxiety as they are learning how to manage their OCD. As their symptoms improve, they may gradually decrease their medications.

Self-Treatment

Ultimately, the goal for people with OCD is to learn to self-treat their symptoms. It is not practical for most people to attend therapy every day, but a person with OCD can expect to have intrusive thoughts or impulses every day. Psychiatrist Jeffrey Schwartz developed a four-step self-treatment plan to overcome OCD. The four-step program

When Intensive Treatment Is Needed

Most people with OCD find outpatient therapy to be successful. Outpatient therapy, often conducted one or two times a week, does not require an overnight stay and is suitable for people who are not in a crisis situation. A typical session lasts forty-five to sixty minutes. When regular outpatient therapy isn't enough, the following programs are recommended for more extreme cases of OCD:

- Intensive outpatient programs (IOPs) feature longer sessions of about ninety minutes. They are conducted several days a week for a specific period of time, such as four to six weeks. These programs may include group therapy, family therapy, and/or support groups.

- Patients who have not found success through IOPs may find help in a residential treatment center. Patients live at the treatment center and receive care around the clock. These programs are very structured and offer CBT with an emphasis on E/RP. They practice group and individual treatment, medication treatment, and family therapy. Patients are permitted to leave the grounds for additional therapy opportunities and recreation.

- When a person with OCD is at risk of hurting himself or others, has become severely malnourished, or is experiencing suicidal thoughts, he should seek emergency care at a hospital.

has been so successful that many mental health professionals have implemented the program in their own practices. The four steps are relabel, reattribute, refocus, and revalue.

Learning to recognize obsessive thoughts and compulsive urges and relabeling them as such is the first step in self-treatment. Understanding the brain's role in directing one's thinking is essential, because when a person has an intrusive thought or an overwhelming urge, he will then have the knowledge to identify it as being symptomatic of his disorder. Jeremy, who struggled with checking compulsions, kept a notepad with him that said "caudate nucleus" to remind him he had a brain problem. He said, "Once the pain had a name, the pain wasn't as bad."[46] Relabeling is deliberate and forces a person to acknowledge his thoughts even if doing so causes him discomfort.

Schwartz describes the importance of being mindful in how one relabels. Relabeling is not simply saying to oneself, "It's not me—it's my OCD." Instead he gives examples of how to accurately relabel. He says, "'I don't *think* or *feel* that my hands are dirty; rather, I'm having an *obsession* that my hands are dirty." "I don't feel the *need* to check that lock; rather I'm having a *compulsive urge* to check that lock.'"[47]

Psychiatrist John March tells his younger patients to rename their OCD. He encourages them to give it a name to reflect how it annoys them. He said, "By naming it for what it is you make it separate from you. Having made it 'not you,' you can hold it out away from yourself, see it clearly for what it is—just a hiccup that has no particular meaning or value—and deal with it skillfully so it goes away and stops bothering you."[48] Some examples of names kids have given their OCD are Mr. Nag, Neat Freak, and Math Nerd. For younger kids, naming their OCD makes it easier for them to talk about and explain how they are feeling when they may not have the developmental skills to do so otherwise. A six-year-old girl called her

> "By naming it for what it is you make it separate from you. Having made it 'not you,' you can hold it out away from yourself, see it clearly for what it is—just a hiccup that has no particular meaning or value—and deal with it skillfully so it goes away and stops bothering you."[48]
>
> —John March, psychiatrist

OCD Noisy. She explained to her doctor how she felt about her OCD while attempting to practice E/RP. "Noisy hurt my feelings this week. Noisy doesn't like chewing noises. I asked my dad [not] to chew really loud at dinner, and it made me really upset when he wouldn't stop even when Mom told him it was too hard for me."[49] This six-year-old may not have had the verbal skills to explain how she was feeling if she hadn't renamed her OCD.

In the second step, reattributing allows the person to place the blame where it belongs—on OCD. By relabeling and reattributing, she is acknowledging that her obsessions and compulsions are the symptoms of a medical condition and she herself is not responsible for her thoughts and urges. The person learns she has a glitch in her brain when her brain gets stuck on an OCD thought pattern—it is not some kind of failing on her part, or something to be ashamed of.

The third step is refocusing. When a person with OCD is bombarded with thoughts or urges, she needs to do something to redirect her focus. This is the action step in the four-step process. It is not enough for the person to admit she has an illness and affirm that it's not her fault. Now she needs to actively change her behavior.

This is the step when she unsticks her brain. Her brain is telling her to do something, but she needs to refocus her attention on another behavior for as long as possible. The goal is to wait fifteen minutes. It is important for the person to choose a behavior that gives her pleasure. After fifteen minutes, the troublesome thoughts will likely begin to fade. Fifteen minutes might be too difficult in the beginning, and she may be unable to last that long. The more she practices refocusing, however, the easier it will become. As time passes and these steps become second nature, she may not need to spend so much time refocusing.

While refocusing her behavior, a person can choose to do something physical, such as playing catch, or something sedentary, such as playing a video game. The key is that the person's mind is actively focused on something she enjoys. She should not be mulling over OCD thoughts or worrying about things that are unrealistic. By not giving in to her temptations, she will decrease her compulsions over time.

Anna, a philosophy student, described the third step as the most difficult. She said, "Refocus was essential to my recovery, but it was a very difficult step to learn. Waiting is about the last thing you want to do when life itself seems to be hinging on whether a compulsion is performed. Distracting myself by doing something else helped."[50]

The final step in the four-step process is to revalue. Once the first three steps are in place, a person with OCD is able to revalue her situation with clarity. Revaluing makes the person be intentional and reflective in her thinking. Being reflective allows her to anticipate obsessions. She knows what to expect from the disorder, and therefore she isn't surprised when an obsession returns. She knows she cannot stop her thoughts from happening, but she has the power to control how she reacts. She learns not to beat herself up for setbacks or bad thoughts because she knows her disorder is the root cause of them.

By revaluing her thoughts, the person with OCD can reflect on her disorder almost from an outside perspective. Anna said, "Once I learned to identify my OCD symptoms as OCD, rather than as 'important' content-laden thoughts that had to be deciphered for their deep meaning, I was partially freed from OCD. . . . I no longer get suckered into obsessing or acting compulsively, as I did before."[51]

Long-Term Treatment and Relapse Prevention

When a person with OCD is approaching the end of treatment, he will begin discussing relapse prevention with his therapist. James Claiborn, an expert with the International OCD Foundation, explains, "A relapse is defined as a return to the same level of symptoms as before treatment. . . . A lapse would represent a partial or brief return of some symptoms."[52] Experiencing a lapse does not mean that a relapse is inevitable.

> "Once I learned to identify my OCD symptoms as OCD, rather than as 'important' content-laden thoughts that had to be deciphered for their deep meaning, I was partially freed from OCD. . . . I no longer get suckered into obsessing or acting compulsively, as I did before."[51]
>
> —Anna, woman with OCD

When a person with OCD concludes his therapy, he will likely have fewer intrusive thoughts than before therapy. However, it is perfectly normal for every person, including people who do not have OCD, to have intrusive thoughts. What the person does with those thoughts will make the difference between a lapse and a relapse.

If a person has an intrusive thought and engages in a ritual because of it, then he is experiencing a lapse. A lapse provides an

OCD patients can benefit from maintaining a strong social support system. Strong personal relationships can give a patient extra support during a lapse.

important learning opportunity. For example, a person with a numbers obsession might find herself struggling while playing Legos with her son, realizing she was doing more counting than playing. This can either lead her to a relapse where she returns to acting out her compulsions, or she can think about what triggered this response, evaluate her behavior, and make a plan for next time.

An important part of therapy is learning to expect lapses and putting a plan in place to deal with them. Preparing for high-risk situations will help the person with OCD succeed when he is on his own. For example, if a person with intrusive thoughts about hurting himself is invited to a movie that he knows will contain violence, he can anticipate that the movie might trigger troubling thoughts. By preparing to confront those thoughts and manage them appropriately, he can participate in this social activity rather than avoiding it.

Some people with OCD like to schedule regular follow-up appointments with their therapists as a way of maintaining their progress. Others prefer to see their therapist only as needed. Whatever the patient decides about frequency of visits, it is imperative that she continue self-care at home to safeguard her mental health. Opening up to loved ones for additional support will also help ensure success. One woman spent years suffering from her symptoms, hiding her disorder from everyone she knew and avoiding professional help. After finally seeking help, she admitted, "My big mistake was that I thought I had to fix my problem myself. I had false pride. I did not want anyone to see my shame."[53]

Obsessive compulsive disorder is a lifelong brain disorder, but it can be managed. Many people with the disorder learn to live fulfilling lives despite their illness. Lizzy S. exhibited signs of OCD at age eight, and she lived without treating her condition into adulthood. Her anxiety peaked whenever she went through major life transitions. After a prolonged episode of losing weight, not sleeping, and being unable to concentrate at work, Lizzy found a therapist who helped her turn her life around. Says Lizzy, "The biggest lesson I have learned . . . is that OCD is a disorder that I need to accept as part of my life for the long haul and continue to manage. For the periods of time when I am feeling well, and stress is low, I do just fine. When stress is higher I have my struggles but have learned to manage much better." She adds, "I hope my story gives others hope as you can live a completely happy and fulfilling life even with OCD. I am living proof."[54]

SOURCE NOTES

INTRODUCTION: TWO STORIES OF OCD

1. National Institute of Mental Health, *Obsessive-Compulsive Disorder*, January 2016. www.nimh.nih.gov.

2. Lee Fitzgibbons and Cherlene Pedrick, *Helping Your Child with OCD*. Oakland: New Harbinger, 2003, p. 19.

3. Quoted in Jared Douglas Kant, Martin Franklin, and Linda Wasmer Andrews, *The Thought That Counts: A Firsthand Account of One Teenager's Experience with Obsessive-Compulsive Disorder*. Oxford, UK: Oxford, 2008, p. 10.

4. Tamar E. Chansky, *Freeing Your Child from Obsessive-Compulsive Disorder*. New York: Crown, 2000, p. 22.

5. John S. March and Christine M. Benton, *Talking Back to OCD: The Program That Helps Kids and Teens to Say "No Way"—and Parents Say "Way to Go."* New York: Guilford, 2007. p. 9.

CHAPTER 1: WHAT IS OCD?

6. *Talking Back to OCD*, p. 18.

7. Charles H. Elliott, "Negative Reinforcement: It Isn't What You Think It Is," *PsychCentral,* February 3, 2012. blogs.psychcentral.com.

8. Quoted in *Freeing Your Child from Obsessive-Compulsive Disorder*, p. 37.

9. *Talking Back to OCD*, p. 19.

10. *Helping Your Child with OCD*, p. 95.

11. Quoted in Kristin McMurran, "A Psychiatrist Explores the Cause—and Treatment—of Those Tormenting, Obsessive-Compulsive Urges," *People,* March 13, 1989. www.people.com.

12. Quoted in *Freeing Your Child from Obsessive-Compulsive Disorder*, p. 13.

13. Quoted in *Freeing Your Child from Obsessive-Compulsive Disorder*, p. 139.

14. *Freeing Your Child from Obsessive-Compulsive Disorder*, p. 108.

15. *Talking Back to OCD*, p. 45.

CHAPTER 2: OCD SYMPTOMS AND DIAGNOSIS

16. Quoted in Steven Reinberg, "Prenatal Factors May Raise Child's Risk for OCD," *WebMD*, October 6, 2016. www.webmd.com.

17. Anxiety and Depression Association of America, *What Does Not Cause OCD*, n.d. adaa.org.

18. Harold S. Koplewicz, *It's Nobody's Fault: New Hope and Help for Difficult Children and Their Parents*. New York: Times Books, 1996, pp. 95–96.

19. *Freeing Your Child from Obsessive-Compulsive Disorder*, p. 44.

20. Quoted in Judith L. Rapoport, *The Boy Who Couldn't Stop Washing: The Experience and Treatment of Obsessive-Compulsive Disorder*. New York: Plume, 1990, pp. 21–22.

21. Quoted in *Freeing Your Child from Obsessive-Compulsive Disorder*, p. 38.

22. Quoted in "New Personal Story: Who Am I? A Student with OCD and Anxiety," *International OCD Foundation*, April 8, 2016. kids.iocdf.org.

23. Diance [last name withheld], "Living With OCD: One Woman's Story." *Anxiety and Depression Association of America,* n.d. https://adaa.org.

24. *Freeing Your Child from Obsessive-Compulsive Disorder*, p. 24.

25. Stanford Medicine, *Obsessive-Compulsive and Related Disorders: Treatment*, 2018. ocd.stanford.edu.

26. *Helping Your Child with OCD*, p. 34.

27. P. Mavrogiorgou et al., "Help-Seeking Behavior and Pathways to Care for Patients with Obsessive-Compulsive Disorders." *PubMed.gov,* September 2015. www.ncbi.nlm.nih.gov.

SOURCE NOTES CONTINUED

CHAPTER 3: THE IMPACT OF OCD

28. Quoted in *Freeing Your Child from Obsessive-Compulsive Disorder*, p. 46.

29. Quoted in *Freeing Your Child from Obsessive-Compulsive Disorder*, p. 38.

30. Quoted in *It's Nobody's Fault*, p. 103.

31. *Helping Your Child with OCD*, p. 37.

32. Angie [last name withheld], "My Sibling Has OCD," *OCD in the Family*, August 19, 2014. ocdinthefamily.wordpress.com.

33. Denise Egan Stack, "Family Involvement in OCD," *OCD Massachusetts*, July 2013. www.ocdmassachusetts.org.

34. Quoted in Jill Berkowicz and Ann Myers, "Working with Parents to Make 'Outside-the-Box' Learners Successful," *Education Week,* June 2017. www.edweek.org.

35. Quoted in "Kids with Obsessive-compulsive Disorder Bullied More Than Others, Study Shows," *ScienceDaily,* August 16, 2006. www.sciencedaily.com.

36. Janet Singer, "Educating Teacher and Students about OCD," *PsychCentral,* n.d. psychcentral.com.

37. *The Thought That Counts*, pp. 68–69.

38. Quoted in Danielle Page, "5 Women Share the Moment They Realized They Had OCD," *Women's Health,* January 15, 2018. www.womenshealthmag.com.

39. Kylie Cloke, "Kylie's OCD Story," *OCD UK,* 2010. www.ocduk.org.

40. Quoted in "OCD—The Consequences and Impact on Our Life," *OCD UK*, November 10, 2016. www.ocduk.org.

41. American Psychiatric Association, *What Is Depression?* January 2017. www.psychiatry.org.

42. *It's Nobody's Fault*, p. 99.

CHAPTER 4: TREATMENT FOR OCD

43. Ben Martin, "In-Depth: Cognitive Behavioral Therapy," *Psych Central*, July 17, 2016. www.psychcentral.com.

44. Quoted in Janet Singer and Seth J. Gillihan, *Overcoming OCD: A Journey to Recovery.* Lanham, MD: Rowman & Littlefield, 2017, p. 152.

45. *It's Nobody's Fault,* p. 102.

46. Quoted in Jeffrey M. Schwartz and Beverly Beyette. *Brain Lock: Free Yourself from Obsessive-Compulsive Behavior.* New York: Harper, 2016, pp. 15–16.

47. *Brain Lock*, p. 11.

48. *Talking Back to OCD*, p. 92.

49. *Talking Back to OCD*, p. 186.

50. Quoted in *Brain Lock*, p. 87.

51. Quoted in *Brain Lock*, p. 102.

52. James Claiborn, "Relapse Prevention in the Treatment of OCD," *International OCD Foundation*, n.d. iocdf.org.

53. Quoted in *Brain Lock*, p. 29.

54. Lizzy S. [last name withheld], "My Battle with Obsessive Compulsive Disorder," *BeyondOCD.org,* n.d. www.beyondocd.org.

FOR FURTHER RESEARCH

BOOKS

Keith Jones, ed., *Anxiety Disorders Sourcebook*. Detroit: Omnigraphics, 2018.

Jared Douglas Kant et al., *The Thought That Counts: A Firsthand Account of One Teenager's Experience with Obsessive-Compulsive Disorder*. Oxford, UK: Oxford, 2008.

Martin L. Kutscher et al., *Kids in the Syndrome Mix of ADHD, LD, Autism Spectrum, Tourette's, Anxiety and More!* London: Jessica Kingsley, 2014.

Jeffrey M. Schwartz and Beverly Beyette, *Brain Lock: Free Yourself from Obsessive-Compulsive Behavior*. New York: Harper Perennial, 2016.

Janet Singer and Seth Gillihan, *Overcoming OCD: A Journey to Recovery*. Lanham, MD: Rowman & Littlefield, 2017.

INTERNET SOURCES

James Claiborn, "Relapse Prevention in the Treatment of OCD," *International OCD Foundation*, June 25, 2014. iocdf.org.

Rebecca Gladding, "You Are Not Your Brain," *Psychology Today*, June 9, 2011. www.psychologytoday.com.

Aureen Pinto Wagner, "Obsessive Compulsive Disorder in Children and Teenagers," *International OCD Foundation*, 2009. iocdf.org.

WEBSITES

Anxiety and Depression Association of America (ADAA)
adaa.org

The ADAA is an international nonprofit organization that educates the public about anxiety and depression disorders. It also supports research and professional training related to these disorders.

International OCD Foundation
iocdf.org

The International OCD Foundation exists to provide support for those living with OCD by disseminating information on effective treatments and confronting the stigma surrounding mental health issues.

National Institute of Mental Health (NIMH)
www.nimh.nih.gov

NIMH is the primary federal agency charged with researching mental disorders. Its mission is to promote better understanding and treatment of mental illnesses by fostering research that leads to prevention, recovery, and cure.

OCD Youth
www.ocdyouth.org

OCD Youth exists to offer support to people under the age of twenty-five who are affected by OCD. It is led by nine young people who have OCD. Activities include maintaining a collaborative website and social media channels; sharing articles, videos, and other resources; and organizing trips and meet-up opportunities.

INDEX

American Psychiatric Association, 53
Anna, 66–67
anorexia nervosa, 55
anxiety
   generalized anxiety disorder
      (GAD), 30
   presence in OCD, 9, 12–14, 16–18,
      26, 28–30, 35, 47–48, 52, 54,
      59–60, 62, 69
Anxiety and Depression Association
   of America, 28

Baxter, Lew, 48
brain involvement
   caudate nucleus, 24–25, 63
   neurotransmitters, 26, 60
   orbitofrontal cortex, 24–26
   thalamus, 24–26
brain lock, 19, 26

Chansky, Tamar, 9, 21, 30, 37
Claiborn, James, 67
compulsions
   checking, 12, 32, 36, 40, 47, 54,
      63, 64
   cleaning, 15–16, 53
   counting, 13, 15, 33, 47, 68
   hoarding, 12, 34–36, 45, 60
   repeating, 12–14 50
   symmetry, 12, 32, 55
   washing, 12–15, 18, 19, 26, 37, 50,
      53–54, 58–59

depression, 26, 28, 29, 53
*Diagnostic and Statistical Manual
   of Mental Health Disorders
   (DSM-5)*, 37
Diane, 33
drugs used in treatment
   selective serotonin reuptake
      inhibitors (SSRIs), 60, 62
   serotonin-norepinephrine reuptake
      inhibitors (SNRIs), 60, 62

Elliott, Charles, 14–15
Emma (fictional character), 6–9

family issues
   effect of OCD on family life,
      40–47
   effect of OCD on marriage, 44
   effect of OCD on siblings, 45–47
   OCD in children, 40–42
   OCD in parents, 51–53
   OCD in teens, 41–42
fear
   physical symptoms, 17
   role in OCD, 8, 12, 14–18, 22,
      30–31, 35, 40, 52–53, 55, 59, 62
Fitzgibbons, Lee, 8, 18, 28, 38,
   44–45

individualized education plan (IEP),
   49–50
International OCD Foundation
   (IOCDF), 38

Jacob, 50
Jake, 29

Kant, Jared, 51
Koplewicz, Harold, 29, 61–62
Kylie, 52–53

Leckman, James, 27
Lizzy S., 69

Mandel, Howie, 20
March, John, 9, 11, 15, 23, 64
Marla, 51
Martin, Ben, 57
Morgan, 33

National Institute of Mental Health, 7

obsessions
   cleanliness, 19, 26, 43, 48
   counting and numbers, 13, 15, 33, 47, 55, 68
   doubting, 32–33
   fear of contamination, 4–5, 8–9, 17–18, 20, 30, 40, 45, 49, 52–55, 58
   fear of driving, 21–22, 31
   fear of injuring someone, 31
   hoarding, 34–36
   need for symmetry, 6, 12, 32, 55
   religion (scrupulosity), 33
   sexual thoughts, 35

obsessive-compulsive disorder (OCD)
   academic concerns, 40, 47–50
   age at onset, 12, 23, 38, 41
   avoidance as coping mechanism, 17–18, 22, 31, 44
   brain disorder, 9, 11, 19, 23–26, 48, 51, 56, 63–65, 69
   comorbidities, 29
   cycle, 9, 14–18
   definition, 7
   diagnosis, 10, 28, 37–39
   effect on sleep, 42, 54, 69
   effects of stress, 27–28, 42, 44, 50, 52, 69
   gender differences, 23
   genetic links, 23, 27
   incidence, 23
   negative reinforcement, 14
   risk factors, 27–29
   rituals, 9, 14, 17, 29, 30, 32, 35, 37, 42–44, 46, 50, 52, 54, 58, 67
   self-image, 15, 39, 51, 53
   social impact, 50–51
obsessive-compulsive spectrum disorders
   body dysmorphic disorder (BDD), 36
   body focused repetitive behaviors (BFRBs), 29, 36
   hoarding disorder (HD), 36

INDEX CONTINUED

PANDAS, 28
PANS, 28

Rapoport, Judith, 18

Schwartz, Jeffrey, 26, 48, 62–67
Singer, Janet, 50–51
Stack, Denise Egan, 47
Stanford University School of
    Medicine, 37–38
Storch, Eric, 50
Susie, 19

treatment
    of children, 61
    cognitive behavioral therapy,
        56–58, 61–62
    exposure and response prevention
        (E/RP), 58–60, 62
    habit reversal therapy (HRT), 60
    intensive outpatient programs, 63
    medication, 60–62
    relapse prevention, 67–69
    residential options, 63
    self-treatment, 62–67
Trey (fictional character), 4–5,
    7–9

Yale-Brown Obsessive Compulsive
    Scale, 39

IMAGE CREDITS

Cover: © pathdoc/Shutterstock Images

5: © Anthony Rosenberg/iStockphoto

6: © Andrey Popov/iStockphoto

8: © Anton Watman/Shutterstock Images

11: © Agent Penguin/Shutterstock Images

13: © Monkey Business Images/Shutterstock Images

16: © MikhailAzarov/Shutterstock Images

22: © Alexandra Rotanova/Shutterstock Images

25: © joshya/Shutterstock Images

31: © Constantine Pankin/Shutterstock Images

34: © Evgeny Pylayev/Shutterstock Images

36: © Red Line Editorial

41: © George Rudy/Shutterstock Images

43: © Yakobchuk Viacheslav/Shutterstock Images

46: © Iakov Filimonov/Shutterstock Images

49: © Monkey Business Images/Shutterstock Images

52: © SpeedKingz/Shutterstock Images

54: © Stock-Asso/Shutterstock Images

57: © fizkes/Shutterstock Images

68: © wavebreakmedia/Shutterstock Images

ABOUT THE AUTHOR

Michelle Garcia Andersen was a teacher for several years. She loved teaching kids to read, and now she loves writing books for kids to read. Michelle has lived in Oregon most of her life and is a graduate of the University of Oregon and Pacific University. She loves reading, writing, and spending time outdoors with her husband and three kids.